THE TRUE STORY OF

CHRISTMAS

This book is a gift for

(aunt)
Kat

from

Slade Overcash Trey

THE TRUE STORY OF
CHRISTMAS

By Nell Navillus

~

Illustrated by Allan Eitzen

Published by Sweetwater Press, Birmingham, Alabama.

Printed in Italy

Library of Congress Cataloging-in-Publication Data
Navillus, Nell
The true story of Christmas / by Nell Navillus ; illustrated by Allan Eitzen.
p. cm.
Summary: A simple retelling of the Nativity story, describing the birth
of Jesus, the special visitors who came to honor him, and the celebration
of the event as Christmas.
ISBN 1-58173-147-7 (hardcover)
1. Jesus Christ — Nativity — Juvenile literature. [1. Jesus Christ — Nativity.
2. Bible stories — N.T. 3. Christmas.] I. Eitzen, Allan, ill. II. Title.
BT315.2.N38 1998
232.92—dc21   98-35531
                          CIP
                          AC

THE TRUE STORY OF
CHRISTMAS

A long time ago in the land of Judea,

a man named Joseph

led his wife Mary,

riding on a donkey,

into a town called Bethlehem.

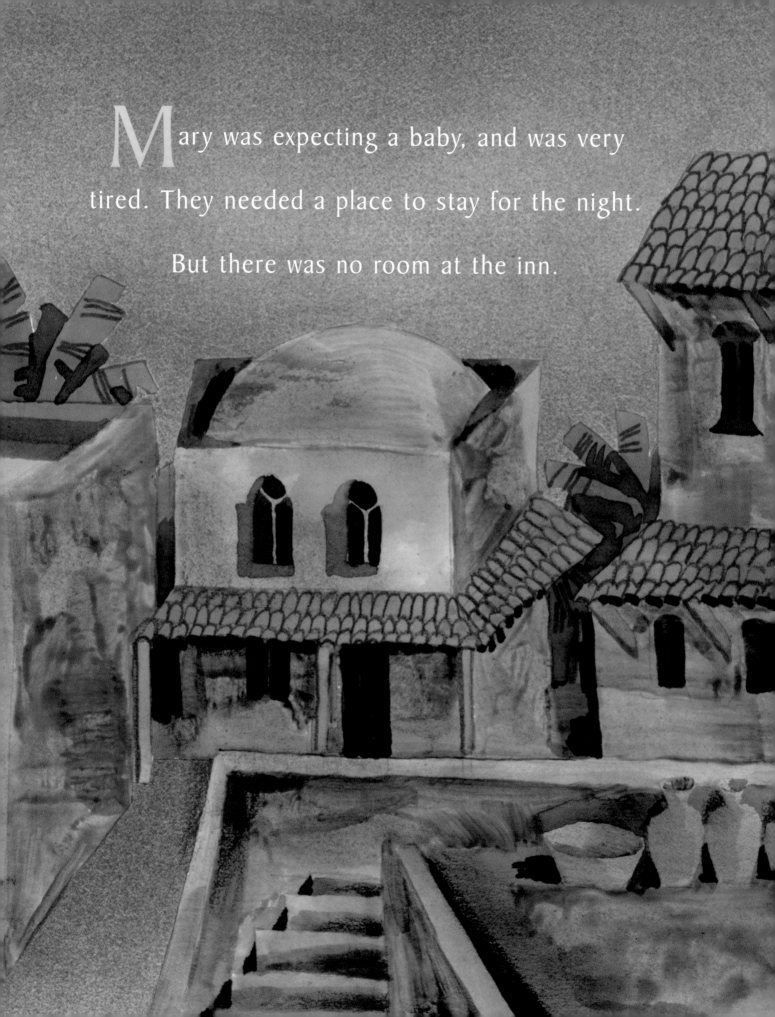

Mary was expecting a baby, and was very tired. They needed a place to stay for the night.

But there was no room at the inn.

Finally one innkeeper

felt sorry for

Joseph and Mary,

and said they could

stay in his stable.

There Mary gave birth to her baby,

while the animals looked on.

The child was named Jesus

and there was great joy

in the stable that night.

Because Jesus was

a very special child.

That same night,

outside the town,

some shepherds were watching

over their flocks when an angel

came down from heaven.

"Don't be afraid,"

said the angel.

"I bring you wonderful news.

Today in Bethlehem

a Savior has been born,

who is Christ the Lord!"

The angel told the
shepherds where to find
the baby wrapped in cloth
and lying in a manger.
And suddenly there were
angels everywhere, singing
"Glory to God in the
highest, and on earth
peace among men."

Following a beautiful bright star,

the shepherds found their way

to the stable in Bethlehem.

Mary and Joseph were there

with the baby, Jesus,

who lay in the manger.

The shepherds rejoiced,

for as the angels

had promised, they'd found

the Son of God.

Meanwhile three kings

in a far-off land

saw the same beautiful star,

shining in the East.

The kings knew

the star meant

God had sent

something special

to all mankind.

Mounting their camels and bearing

rich gifts, they too set off

to follow the star.

When the kings arrived at the lowly stable

in Bethlehem they found the baby Jesus,

surrounded by his family, the shepherds,

and the stable animals.

The kings sank to their knees

offering gifts they had brought

to the newborn king.

God had sent his only son,

Jesus Christ, to be born

in a manger in Bethlehem.

Jesus would save the world

from sin and offer

life everlasting to

people everywhere.

Forever after, that special day

in Bethlehem would be celebrated

as Christmas, the birthday of Jesus

Christ Our Lord.

And that

is the true story

of Christmas.